Ravi feels good.
He scored a hat trick!

He creeps into the room and sees a man.

Then zigzags high and low.

Ravi gets over his shock and relaxes. He begins to quiz Carl.

So have you been here long, Carl?

Yes. I've been stuck here for years. I was a goalkeeper …

Carl explains sadly how he has been waiting so long to be set free.